At Durgan

Poems 2012 to 2016

by

David Pike

2

This edition was first published in year 2017 by Ligden Publishers.

Ligden Publishers, 34 Lineacre, Swindon, Wiltshire, UK, SN5 6DA

Email: pulsar.ed@btopenworld.com

www.pulsarpoetry.com

Youtube: PulsarPoet

Twitter: https://twitter.com/pulsarpoet

ISBN: 978-0-9570254-6-2

Author Note

David Pike, (DP), founded and has edited Pulsar Poetry Magazine, (now Pulsar Poetry Webzine – www.pulsarpoetry.com), from year 1994 to the present day. Over a course of years DP's own work has been published in various poetry magazines, newspapers, books and webzines. DP remains a keen poet/writer/editor. A list of his publications may be viewed within the covers of this book.

NB:

You may also view 'live' versions of the poems via YouTube via the PulsarPoet channel.

Foreword

How would I categorize this collection of poems? Honest? Realistic? Welcoming? Eclectic? Approachable? Distinctive? Let's have a look together, before you yourselves make up your own minds.

David Pike's 50-poem collection comprises a number of themes, with an emphasis on observation and description, yet with one authentic voice knitting them together into one viable entity.

David Pike builds up his poem-pictures bit by bit, word by word, image by image, association by association, imbuing his work with a rhythmic, echoing motion and tone.

He has a great eye for landscapes, and views them very much with the eye of a painter, as in VERDANT GREEN, where he writes of the 'canvas' being engraved by a 'southerly road', and 'meandering tracks/and chalk trails'.

One particular sequence of poems etches scenes of shorelines and landscapes, with a lingering, vocal sense of the poet's self and identity, as well as taut, observational imagery, as in AT DURGAN – SEPTEMBER 28th

2012: 'a thousand limpets/clinging to granite stones/like discarded chewing gum'.

Poems such as HELFORD TREES paint, or draw a picture, as David builds up a kaleidoscope of an autumnal scene, adding greater colour and widening the view, as extra elements of the scene are described, with 'Autumnal leaves/in varying shades', and trees 'tumbling, tumbling/from tidal creeks' performing a fully etched 'brackish dance'.

These are quite lyrical pieces, yet often imbued with a jolting tone, as of an eye focussing on different sections of the scene, or maybe the view from a car snaking its way through its parts (as in SALTHROP). This is linked to the sense of movement integral to the poems, provided by roads, rivers and masses of trees and leaves and the movement within them, or imbued within them by the poet's eye fixing upon and following them.

Other poems muse on life, with a healthy contempt for any form of self-importance and pretension, and exhibit some much appreciated good old-fashioned bashing of the upper classes; some dwell on the process of self-expression; others are an incisive description of people and animals.

My other particular favourites? PERFECTLY CLEAR and its constant refrain 'Not here/anywhere but here', with its jaunty, jokey rendering of our sense of alienation, our inability to really relate to the here-and-now; DOING THE DO, which glorifies the world of 'also-rans', something we can all sympathize with ('Being an also ran/lets you get nowhere/fast...'); and CONTACT, poignant and touching, centred on an old man's isolation and loneliness.

I am proud to have had the opportunity to read this collection prior to publication, and feel sure its readers will share in my pleasure not just in the poems, but in the image of their creator thereby provided, someone of an unfazed disposition who views life and nature with an unprepossessing, undaunted and faithful eye.

Alan Hardy, Whitehill School of English.

Acknowledgements

Many thanks to Alan Hardy and Andrew Barber for their kind help.

I dedicate this book to my wife, Jill, and grandchildren. DP.

Contents

Downland

Sooner or later,
or perhaps
before
the uproar
there was this,
a gentle hiss
of near silence,
a transient place
giving
a certain nuance
of gentleness,
a step back
from the brink
a time for reflection
to contemplate
and make sense;
calmness
in the wake
of constant
input.

Salthrop

In dark winter hours
whilst motoring
atop a minor road
that flops to Basset Down
headlights strobe
bleak open fields
where winds comb
unchecked, to expose
a solitary vehicle;
the cyclone buffets, buffeting
eager to drone
a plaintiff Siren song
luring the driver on
towards the brow
of reflective chevrons
and hilltop eyrie
where two cottages cling
straddling the view
of lowland beads of light
that waver
from the urban sprawl, then
down a gear
to crawl around the double
reservoir bend
then descend sharply

slicing ice
gravity borne, gaining speed
as if drawn by an invisible force
hypnotically, through a dark
engulfing woodland course
that snakes downwards
through Salthrop Wood
slewing, skittering
snaking around a rutted
gravel strewn slope,
brake, brake and
brake again, lights reveal
imagined ghosts
spewing from the mouths
of private roads,
slowing, slowing,
the engine groans
to level ground
heading down
for Hay Lane;

steering for a level plain.

At Durgan – September 28th 2012

The Helford river glides
almost furtively
out to sea, a rippling sheen
of low-tide water
incising a steep valley
of lush fauna and
exotic trees -
brown, burgundy, green;
the reduced flow reveals
floating driftwood flotsam,
abandoned fishing twine
and a thousand limpets
clinging to granite stones
like discarded chewing gum,
fastened home – biding time
for the incoming tide.

We view, as scuba divers scramble
comically
over shoreline stones
and dive into a mix of
river and brine
enjoying sport, passing time

indulging a dying summer song,
but for a while -
with the discovery of a World War II
parachute mine
unexploded, but dangerous still;
and the ensuing hullabaloo. . .

And as the shoreline declines
is quickly submerged
beneath the oncoming tide
I sense a ghostly inshore flotilla
sweeping the line
gently, gently, searching for explosives
below the surface
missing one. . .

carrying out hazardous service.

Helford Trees

Autumnal leaves
in varying shades,
float as strands
of gold and green
in tidal rout,
lap back and forth
drawn gently towards
the estuary mouth.

On opposing banks
Helford trees
stand in ranks
of random splendour,
emerald and tan
fixed, yet
tumbling down
in arrays
of exotic fauna,
tumbling, tumbling
from tidal creeks
to the sea expanse
they adorn the high
and lower shore
to warm the heart

reflected in a brackish dance.

Rendezvous

The motorway hums
a refrain
of many vehicles -
eastbound, westbound
outbound, inbound;
metal endurance boxes
endure, grind or purr
at 70 miles plus per hour,
with somewhere to
flow -
past a host of marker posts
for reasons the occupants know

driven as demand dictates
with miles to devour,
to be somewhere else
and make themselves known
to appear and engage
at a different
hour.

Verdant Green

Looking down
upon verdant sward and trees
it appears akin to an impression
a kind of artist's random dream,
with expressive strokes, splashing
acre upon acre
of green on green
with nearby implied gallop rails
plus meandering tracks
and chalk trails,
while an insistent southerly road
gently inclines, engraves the canvas
with cool precision;
then focussing on and through
a wavering haze
to a misty horizon
of lowland buildings barely seen -
to Wantage town
partially screened from view
by the trees of Chain Hill,
observed from The Ridgeway
on a July day
when the land drew breath
and all was still,
a rolling landscape

of patchwork fields. . .

as a nearby sign
draws the eye from the rural vista
a legend of our time, so far,
"Don't leave valuables
on view
in your car."

Wantage viewed from the Ridgeway, near the road to
Newbury on 13th July 2013

Relics

And so they roamed
stood, stared, walked
and railed
around sarsen stones;
it made their day
to do this,
to commune with something
elemental,
to stand alone,
observing ancient monoliths
immovable objects, relics
there because they are,
bearing no insignia
of religious candour
but vaguely ceremonial, ritualistic -
feelings grown
through natural order
day, night, fire, water, wind
soil, loam,
and time, endless time
stretching from then, now -
seemingly slow
but swifter than
the power
of attention,

as the land commands
we are born, live
come and go
return to soil

for renewed existence
the earth will sow

*

School Photo

A slightly creased, aging photo
of young people, adolescents
students, standing to loose attention
as a frozen view of their generation -
now observed
by an older person
who remembered when
he stood in-place
back row, on the right
snapped in black and white
unassuming, with a hopeful face
staring at a lens.

Voyage

Slowly, very slowly
perhaps even slower
than that
the buoyant structure
slewed gently onwards
across a flat
non-bilious sea.

Progress was made
in degrees, inching
pitching,
bearing towards a remote island promontory –
to navigate and elude rocks
of proven treachery.

No dolphins, sunfish
or basking sharks were on hand
to relieve the ennui
of open deck exhaust fumes
and a featureless sea
but steadily, eventually
the sojourn gained appeal
with slow-time charm and
style –

on docking at
Hugh Town, St Mary's,
of the temperate
Scillonian isles.

*

The Cat

He's outside
and shouting
"m-waa-p, m-waa-p,"
annoyed with all
and sundry
plus this
and that,
making it known –
"m-waa-p, m-waa-p,"

Elmo, the cat.

Climbing the Wall

An octopus
climbed up the inside
of aquarium glass
a bit at a time, holding fast
hauling itself
up a line,
a piece of twine
that minders had purposely left
fastened down,
an intelligent creature
looking out
as we looked in askance,
open mouthed
as it performed a practised dance
of climbing the wall,
looking big
in a small place,
rising with haste
at a rapid rate –

just part of the show,
it went where it had to
go, because it couldn't go
anywhere else,
moving from shelf

to shelf;
with all the time
in the world.

Octopus, seen at the Bluereef Aquarium, Newquay,
Cornwall, July 2012.

*

Feline

Stretched out
at an impossible angle
yet seemingly comfortable
and staring at me
lies a calico cat
orange, white, black
at ease with herself
at ease with everything else,
unblinking, barely moving
unassuming. . .
pawing the fur
of her pelt.

Perfectly Clear

Not here,
anywhere but here,
elsewhere
yeah, elsewhere
but not here -
somewhere undeclared
perhaps austere,
a street, a block
a town away
but not here

you may say
nearby
oh aye, seemingly fine
out of eye-line
not here

I understand
the constant demands
and sympathise
with the many complex strands
of complexity,
and state with no fear
of contradiction,
not here

however, it could be encased
in a space
where it will merge
be appreciated and fall
into line,
and given a period of time
I'm sure it will be fine

but not here.

Clarion of Dawn

The high-pitched wailing-whining,
whinged a droning score
followed by a clattering-clunky sound
as a plastic hose suction
device,
was dragged, protesting
over traffic-worn grease
of a bleached
faun coloured floor.

It was the early clarion call
as vacuums whirred,
ever hungry
to suck-up dust
from the earth's crust,
while cleaners cleaned
wiped a bit
and emptied bins,
bustling around
ill-lit halls
and pre-dawn corridors
of a thousand offices
of a thousand towns,
too early for most
unseen, they move around.

Fog of Dialogue

'There's a lot
to be said about it'
he bled –
falling silent.

'I could talk
about it all day,'
she exclaimed –
as her voice
tailed away.

Followed by a long
drawn-out spell
of nothing expelled
by either party.

'Don't get me started,'
he imparted
looking anxious and vacant
at the same time.

She declined to reply. . .

The Depth They Tread, Loud
Though Lightly Falls

Let me spout you
some incomprehensible bollocks,
it's what expected
you see,
about something obscure
demure
and fleeting
that only a few
will read,
and say they saw
a hidden meaning
a slant, a trace
or leaning
towards something
that might just be,
to plumb the depths
of unfathomable worth
and say they were the first
to agree,
but in reality
it's a load of bollocks
a case of Betty Swallocks
that only the deepest

of deep thinkers,
undoubtedly
fail to perceive.

Doing the Do

Being an also ran
is part of a
cunning plan
to be there but
invisible,
to the highly
visible,
who tend
to only see themselves
as they function
through a wealth
of unbridled
I am I am,
thrashing around
for the next bout
of getting somewhere,
and on getting there
stress
for something else.

Being an also ran
lets you get nowhere
fast, ignored and
in a state of impasse,
doing the do,

while winners
thunder past.

Glint

'One may boot
one up the bum,'
she expressed, regally restrained
less than impressed
with my portrayal
of her walking with a gammy knee,
a condition that was proving a test,
being far from ideal.

A moment of silence, then
'violence is never
the answer,'
I implied, stoically,
perhaps philosophically – hopefully.

'Maybe not,' she replied
with a glint in her eyes,
'but I think it will do
for me.'

Oozing Clout

The essential
existential
piece
of modern art
lay fastened
to a board – flat out,
more expensive
than anything
that had gone
before
but not outlandishly
so,
there to be admired
interpreted, adored
a red elastic band
glued to a sea of noir
representing the
inner self,
the very meaning of
life
or something else,
or an elastic band
stuck on felt
for those less demonstrative
or easily bored.

Stepping Out

Into the dark nothingness
of zilch
there ventured
three sponsored celebs,
fully indentured
with little else to do
and nothing to prove
other than they are
vacuous,
bathed in an exultant hue
of media madness. . .

Stepping out
they step
onwards, backwards
forwards, outwards, inwards
into a review
of cameras,
that focus on the living stew
so that many
may be
fed.

Again, and Every Now and Then

And it all
comes down
to this. . .
not what was anticipated
by a long chalk,
not now, not here;
the timing's all wrong
that much is clear
if you could time it
at all,
at any time
near

a minor tremor, flicker
disturbs the norm
as a thought of
a thought
of a thought before
stumbles about,
searching, converging
in haste to
fall
and crush
my pint of beer,
gravity drawn

to present its ugly head,
by dint of sheer
absurdity.

Intrinsically Bad

This poem
contains explicit material
and should only
be read by
persons of 18 years
of age or older
and includes many
references to things
which entice, solicit, smoulder
and are disgustingly rude,
crude, and unsightly.

Do not read
if you are of a timid, shy
or nervous disposition
because this stuff
has all of the above
with a bit more thrown in
of an erotic, suggestive
ouch elected
yaroo! - thank you
corrective, bothered,
slobbered,
chafed and bruised
nature.

So, WARNING
don't read this poem
as it is intrinsically bad.

Oh, you already have.

There You Have It

I was under the distinct impression
that you feel and suggest
I am less than correct
in this matter
and thus I would, with alacrity
like to impress, quite strongly
you are wrong, irrefutably
and
that I am in fact
as right as right
on a particularly correct day
and won't be swayed
by undignified patter
looks of dismay, arguments
or confrontational scenes;
it is as it is
hrmmph, and I will say this
do yourself a favour
admonish yourself
consider your behaviour
and acknowledge along the way
forever and a bit longer
that my opinion wins.
So there you have it,
now kindly walk away.

Rumble Strips

Thrusting -
thrustingly
they like to thrust
new things upon us;
mandatory, no choice
things,
all done thrustingly
"here, 'ave it
with no returns,"
the usual way
and typically depicted
for the common good,
where the effected
are allowed to comment
but effectively
have no say.

Unlike Rhubarb

Don't confuse the muse
with anything useful
it's too obtuse
for that,
it's an unexpected thing
not a fixture -
think feline, a supine cat
reclining, sunning itself
when a fly unexpectedly
comes along
to add interest to the mixture;
the muse is something
you wish you had
as a matter of course
on tap,
but unlike rhubarb
it cannot be forced;
it's a kind of
heady elixir
a rush, a grab
that spreads colour
to a monochrome picture
to bring the mind alive,
a kind of seismic stab
that unfurls an iridescent

world
there on your pad
and sends mediocrity
to another region.

To Know

There was a lingering doubt,
not one that rushed about
bumping into things,
no
it was a lingering doubt,
a doubt that remained
in a back room
sipping wine, swilling stout
biding its time
hanging around,
as a lingering doubt -
niggling, chipping slowly away
wearing down cerebral tissue,
gristle,
to leave a barb, ingrained,
holding on, holding fast
changing tack, but always
somewhere close at hand,
there, or there about -

a lingering doubt.

Contact

Old Arnold
closed the door.
The annoying knocking sound
revealed no-one there;
at least, not anymore,
they'd either run away
gone to ground
or hadn't been there
in the first place,
it appeared a jape
he realised that
but would've
liked to have seen them
just the same,
perhaps face to face
because then the game
would have subtly changed
become something else -
because old Arnold
lived alone
rattling around
the derelict shell,
being the only ghost
in the house.

Moving

Down in a cellar
something stirred,
something that shouldn't
be there
but was there
anyway –
to linger and lurk
unseen
with an ugly smirk
across its face
in a place where
darkness dug a trench
and light paled
to something less
dust fell as velvet
snow
in a recurrent
dream
upon something that
was there
moving, persisting,
existing

but shouldn't have
been.

In Their Own Special Way

Pillocks
not idiots
not imbeciles
or intellectually challenged
just pillocks,
pillocks
not misinformed
unfairly scorned
or reborn again
as something zealous,
just pillocks,
pillocks
dancing along
in their own special way
which seems to say
look at me, the pillock,
pillocks
to the left
pillocks
to the right
always there,
seldom out of sight
day or night,
pillocks.

Bonzo

The ugly looking
attack dog,
on a chain
being led
by a monosyllabic being
who, in the presence
of three other similar beings
between them collectively formed
a single brain. . .
walked with a bow-legged gait
sniffing and snarling
at all creatures in its wake
waiting for a chance
to tear something apart,
and thus

seal its fate. . .

Strong Jelly

Yip yip,
the scrawny weevil kid
shook his fist
spouted a venous diatribe hiss
then ran and hid
behind his older
(and larger)
brother.

He was bold,
but only when in the company
of overgrown others,
a bit like a crab
having a slab to scurry behind,
scuttling, waving a claw
as the tide elapsed

to leave him collapsed and forlorn
looking expectantly
for a punch on the jaw
that should inevitably
befall him.

Against the Grain

She came as a ghastly
old bint
with a matching
leathery git
of an old man,
and they didn't linger
deliberate
or hang around
to spawn a flood
of appalling sprogs,
all unique in
in a way
but chipped
against the grain
from a block of the same
ghastliness

and they lived
in a disparate side of town,
a place
of moronic farts
burnt-out cars
and things torn down,
where they slouched about
in the loud pursuit

of everything that didn't suit
anyone else

and it could be said they excelled
at being ghastly –
ghastly, ghastly,
occasionally arsey,
and ghastly
times twelve.

The Gentle Folk

They like it
not one jot
being told what
to do,
to stand in line
and queue
like others,
because they are
special
you see,
better than you,
more worthy than
me,
and are not inclined
or designed
to comply
with mundane procedures,
and say
they'd rather decline
than mix with ordinary
lay folk,
the vaguely known
grey figures
who should defer
to another place,

and look suitably
assuaged
in the presence
of gentlewomen,
gentlemen, gentle folk

who gently,
gentle over others -

it's how they
cope.

Appearance of. . .

. . .a stereotypical
young bloke
in a hooded coat
hood up;
by default
a dodgy sort,
nothing more.

It's a kind of uniform
purchased
to conform with
others of a same
age,
just a phase
at a moment in time,
not something emblazoned
deep within
when born.

Just a temporary
uniform.

On the Contrary

In a total
non-discriminatory way
it has been observed
and I'd like to say
(but daren't)
that all is not
what it seems,
but, of course
this does not imply
any stilted views, hidden agendas
or schemes
of a disproportionate
nature,
no, everything is in
order
(bit isn't)
though appears more correct
than something completely
in-check,
on a pristine
squeaky clean day . . .

as the whole lot
slips away.

Dud

With a metallic 'clunk'
a pound coin
entered the cheese-cake grin
of the seaside car park
ticket machine -
to be thrown from within
like wallet vomit,
spinning
clattering in the reject
bin.

"You have to enter
your registration number first,"
a young female said, calmly - politely.

"I know," I replied
not generously
and entered my car reg. again.
She hovered near,
overseeing the old dear
who apparently was me.

The same pound coin
was fed to the machine
which spat out the offering

with great alacrity.

"Perhaps the coin's a dud?"
I ventured, slightly unnerved.

"You have to enter your registration number
first," she said, again
in a previously rehearsed patient way.

"I know," I relayed.

Pending Ablutions

The storm approached,
slowly, furtively,
with distant mumbles
and bass note
dissidence,
reverberating indiscreetly,
raking
the silence

no breathing object
cared, or batted
an eyelid
as long as the deluge
came quickly
to expunge the leaden
air
of stifling humidity.

Circling, it circled
as if running scared
of intrusion,
rumbling
a string of half-heard obscenities
of sonic flatulence
that came to nothing –

repeating, drifting, retreating,

hanging around

soaking some other stretch
of land.

Bow Wave

As the old school
leave
the new school
breathes new life
into a tired mechanism,
and,
buoyed by enthusiasm,
inspiration
they approach a known
subject
unhindered by
cynicism,
to see it for
what it is,
and make things
come alive, exist
through verve and
dynamism.

But as time accrues
and adds a bit
more
something new stagnates
to become a chore
paling to the familiar

regular, known,
and the new school
become less enthralled
and unknowingly revert
to the school of before
becoming jaded
bored
by more of the more,
and covertly seek
a means to leave
which given time
they eventually
achieve, to walk
the walk
and pass the new
bright things
as they unwittingly
dance
through a revolving door.

This We know

When the sun went away
late on
at the end of the day –
without fail
they'd go to bed,
and it has to be said
they were quite predictable
in this.

Never Has My Flabber Been So Gasted

It begged the question
to help solve the conundrum
about what was what
what wasn't, isn't
and never has been,
or, occasionally
on a Saturday afternoon
in a small town
due south west of East Ham
on the 4th June
every other year
sometimes in the morning
but mainly during the afternoon,
is seen to be
something outrageously
astonishingly, heinously
startlingly

ordinary.

National Insurance

The tide rolled out,
well, not exactly rolled,
it tugged and surged
splurged a bit
taking all sorts of crap
with it;
and the moon relaxed
having done its job
took a nap, took time off
until later in the day
when it shoved the whole lot
back
by gravitational sway,
to gurgle and slap
around boats that were
trapped
in glistening mud
of the tidal creek;
and surprisingly the moon wasn't bored
by this daily occurrence
having a job for life
with an index linked pension
and free National Insurance.

Mrs Malaprop

Meanwhile. . .
in the expensive houses
at the rear of the posh park
that's lined with an imposing
display of ever popular
poplar trees
Mrs Malaprop wheezed
to make herself a pot of tea
of the exclusive kind
and relaxed, sat down
to unwind, drain away
the day
in a recliner chair,
imbibing the infusion
without a thinking care, sipped
sipped. . .
not really knowing
why she breathed, who she was
or why she was
there.

Non-Stop

On behalf of,
and at the behest
of others,
I will
with due diligence,
read to you
free-of-charge,
and with nothing owing
my thirty-five minute
non-stop
epic poem,
and I can see
from the glowing
mask of your face
you are intrigued
by the chance
to listen, and perhaps
participate?

What's that you say
perhaps on another day
and, oh. . .
you must be going.

Juxtaposing

In the middle of nowhere,
at a point between there
and a place
less easily discerned
is where we are,
having travelled
a few steps
or far,
but always
with somewhere else
to know.

Moriarty's Party

How super
he's moved him orn
got rid of that party pooper
Justin St. John
who'd connived
'n had the damned impudence
to arrive with a corker,
Miss Blythington-Smythe
and made out 'they were carrying orn,'
which wasn't true
you see she's rather spiffing
being totally blue, through and through
just like me,
and I've got me eye on her
you see
oh yes, what-o;
so good old Caruthers
moved him orn
drove him in the Rolls
to the back of beyond
and left him there,
which didn't seem fair
but was entirely appropriate,
you have to hand it to Caruthers
he says little

and seldom quibbles
when there's a job to be done,
he earns his corn, and then some,
and now the whole party's
come alive old bean
it's me and her
and those in between
dancing splendidly with Miss Blythington-
Smythe
coz she's a bit of alright
although my aunt won't agree,
says she's immoral
which between you and me
is a pleasing trait, har har ha-r,
anyway, gotta go, super show
she relying on me
for a wap-wap-wap
and a woe-de-woe,
so see yar later,
can't be late.

Sojourn You All

Yar – there is
little doubt
you may go far
in a car – you know
one of those automobile
thingeys; perhaps take the Lagonda
for a wander
with a toot-toot, parp-parp
and a rousing something
or other,
as your cravat gently flutters
in the breeze;
you may travel
short distances
up tree-lined drives
of stately piles
owned by stuffy Lord Smithers
and other notable
tweed-clad duffers
with miserable matriarchs
whose daughters are chinless
and as gormless as me,
so we could be a match
for each other
you see.

Well there's a thought,
if it doesn't come to something
it will come to nought.
Yar, so here's to the car
and travels to be.

*

On the High Plains

A herd of steel
shopping trolleys
gallop and graunch
on castor wheels,
sliding, objecting
on a carpark hill,
squealing obscenities
jostling around
wrangling the angles,
juddering ever down
the ASDA prairie,
towards a plastic
corral.

The Flow of Things

And so
into another year,
I shake a fist
at your general
demands
and sneer at
your fortitude,
to think you can
hit me
with something unplanned
and stand back
sniggering
with raised eyebrows -
to appraise what you
may,
start or undo
by way of random
interludes,
or speed up
or slow down
the flow
of things
is all part of
how you go,
stop, start, yes, no

I think I have
the measure of
you.

On Occasion

"During winter
the wind blows
so hard
you have to lean forward
at a slant,
to address the gale,
or be blown
afar
by the squall -
and fall away,"

said distractedly
during a brief interlude,
passing the time of
day;

another Cornish anecdote
from a local resident
to a summer migrant
who was there by arrangement
for a temporary stay.

Wee Small Hours

And by way of
conclusion
I'd like to give
the illusion that
I've achieved something. . .

something to remember
me by
when I'm gone,
a kind of resonance
or residue
to latch onto
and read
in the wee small hours

but it seems from
from your expression
I am misguided
and perhaps
have lapsed into
into the realm
of heady ascension

or failing that,
I'm just out and out,
wrong.

Books by David Pike

Sentinel of the Row, novel, published 1992,
ISBN 0-9520431-0-6 out of print.

On the Ridge, poems, published 1993,
ISBN 0-9520431-1-4

A Cold Night for Norman, short Stories,
published 1994, ISBN 0-9520431-2-2.

A Cold Night for Norman, e-book version,
published 2012, ISBN 978-0-9570254-0-0

In the Mix, poems, published 2007,
ISBN 978-0-9520431-8-8

In the Mix, e-book version,
published 2011, ISBN 978-0-9520431-9-5

Bottomley Steps Out, novel, e-book,
published 2012, ISBN 978-0-9570254-1-7

The Strand, poems, published 2012,
ISBN 978-0-9570254-2-4

The Strand, e-book version, published 2012,
ISBN 978-0-9570254-3-1

Bottomley in Love, novel, e-book,
published 2015, ISBN 978-0-9570254-4-8

Bottomley and the Laird of Liskeard,
novel, e-book, published 2016,
ISBN 978-0-9570254-5-5

At Durgan, poems, published 2017
ISBN 978-0-9570254-6-2